Collins

Easy Learning

Grammar and punctuation practice

Age 5-7

My name is _____.

I am _____ years old.

I go to _____ School.

How to use this book

- Find a quiet, comfortable place to work, away from other distractions.
- Tackle one topic at a time.
- Help with reading the instructions where necessary and ensure your child understands what to do.
- Encourage your child to check their own answers as they complete each activity.
- Discuss your child what they have learnt.
- Let your child return to their favourite pages once they have been completed, to talk about the activities.
- Reward your child with plenty of praise and encouragement.

Special features

- Yellow boxes: Introduce a topic and outline the key grammar or punctuation ideas.
- Red boxes: Emphasise a rule relating to the unit.
- Yellow shaded boxes: Offer advice to parents on how to consolidate your child's understanding.

Useful definitions

Grammar	
Noun	Naming words, e.g. house, dog, kite
Proper noun	A noun that is the name of something, like a person, a day, a month or a place, e.g. Dan, Tuesday, June, India.
Verb	A verb is usually a doing word, e.g. run, jump, write. It tells you what is happening.
Singular	Singular means one.
Plural	Plural means more than one.
Punctuation	
Full stop	A full stop (.) often shows where a sentence ends.
Question mark	A question mark (?) is used at the end of a sentence to show a question has been asked.
Comma	Commas have different uses. In this book they are used to separate items in a list.
Exclamation mark	An exclamation mark (!) is used at the end of a sentence to show shock, surprise, upset or an order.

Published by Collins
An imprint of HarperCollins*Publishers*
77–85 Fulham Palace Road
Hammersmith
London
W6 8JB

Browse the complete Collins catalogue at
www.collins.co.uk

© HarperCollins*Publishers* 2012

10 9 8 7 6 5 4 3

ISBN 978-0-00-746734-1

British Library Cataloguing in Publication Data

A Catalogue record for this publication is available from the British Library

Page layout by Linda Miles, Lodestone Publishing
Illustrated by Kathy Baxendale, Rachel Annie Bridgen, Graham Smith, Andy Tudor
Cover design by Linda Miles, Lodestone Publishing
Cover illustration by Kathy Baxendale
Commissioned by Tammy Poggo
Project managed by Chantal Peacock
Printed and bound by Printing Express, Hong Kong

MIX
Paper from
responsible sources
FSC™ C007454

FSC™ is a non-profit international organisation established to promote the responsible management of the world's forests. Products carrying the FSC label are independently certified to assure consumers that they come from forests that are managed to meet the social, economic and ecological needs of present and future generations, and other controlled sources.

Find out more about HarperCollins and the environment at
www.harpercollins.co.uk/green

Contents

Capital letters

Capital letters:

A B C D E F G H I J K L M

N O P Q R S T U V W X Y Z

Every **sentence** starts with a capital letter.

The cat is asleep.

Q1 Add the missing capital letters.

A B ___ D E F ___ H I J K ___ M

N O ___ Q R ___ T U V W ___ Y Z

Q2 Copy the sentences.
Add the missing capital letters.

it is a hot day.

_____

the dog sat on a cat.

_____

we like sweets.

_____

Capital letters are one of the devices used to help words make sense.

Most sentences end with a **full stop**.

The baby is crying.

Q1 Copy the sentences.
Add the missing full stops.

The pool is fun

_____

A girl plays tennis

_____

Dan walks to school

_____

The hen laid an egg

_____

Q2 Use your own words to finish the sentences.
Remember the full stop.

The cow eats _grass in the field._

The dog barks _loudly in the garden._

The baby smiles _and laughs._

Explain to your child that full stops give a signal to the reader that a pause is needed. Read a short extract without pausing to illustrate the role of the full stops.

Nouns

Nouns are naming words.

gate   flower   grass

Q1 Use the nouns in the box to label the pictures.

| chair | dog | boat | sun | tree | ring |

_____ _____ _____

_____ _____ _____

Q2 Look around you and list the nouns you can see.

How many have you listed?

5 = good   **7** = great   **10** = fantastic

Ask your child to look around the room they are sitting in – list as many nouns as they can find.

Proper nouns

A **proper noun** is a noun that is the name of a person or place.

> **Proper nouns** always start with a capital letter.

Sam lives in **Spain**.

Amy lives in **Australia**.

Q1 Circle the proper nouns.

kite   **Meena**   London   man   **Ben**   torch   **Africa**

Cinderella   Tonkin Road   coat   **pen**   **Mr Atkin**   France

Q2 Answer the questions using a proper noun.
Remember the capital letters.

What is your name? _____

Which town do you live near? _____

Who is your best friend? _____

Who is your teacher? _____

Where did you go on holiday? _____

What is the name of your road? _____

Look in a reading book and ask your child to note the different proper nouns they can find.
Introduce other proper nouns to your child, e.g. family names, street names

Every sentence starts with a **capital letter**.
Most sentences end with a **full stop**.

The bird watches the fish**.**

Q1 Copy the sentences.
Add the missing capital letters and full stops.

it is raining

_____

we love sweets

_____

sam is swimming

_____

Q2 Use these pairs of words to write three of your own sentences.

dog stick   baby food   lion sleep

_____

_____

_____

Ask your child to read aloud a few sentences without capital letters and full stops – this will highlight their need.

Words must be in the right order for **sentences** to make sense.

Grass sheep eat. ✗   Sheep eat grass. ✔

Q1 Write these words in the right order to make a sentence.

Anywhere sleep cats.

_____

Splash the puddles in children.

_____

Car grey is the.

_____

Q2 Use these words to write a sentence.
Remember the capital letter and the full stop.

holiday   we   going

_____

grumpy   teacher

_____

bites   lion   zookeeper

_____

Write some short sentences for your child without capital letters and full stops. Ask them to rewrite them correctly.

Verbs 1

A **verb** is usually a doing word.
It tells us what is happening.

Max **runs** to the finish line.

Q1 Write the verb each picture is showing.

| skiing | cycling | eating | slipping | standing | laughing |

_____   _____   _____

_____   _____   _____

Q2 List some verbs. They must be things you have done today!
(Hint: Have you brushed your teeth?)

How many have you listed?

5 = good   **7** = great   **10** = fantastic

Verbs can be regular or irregular (sing, sang). Although this topic doesn't cover this subject it is worth being aware of it in case your child notices that some verbs are different.

Questions help us find out things.

What is the time?

A question begins with a **capital letter** and ends with a **question mark**.

Q1 Copy and correctly write each question.

where are you going

_____

why is your coat muddy

_____

when can I eat my snack

_____

what is his name

_____

Q2 Write three of your own questions.
(Hint: What have you asked your mum or dad today?)

_____

_____

_____

Challenge your child to think of six different questions in one minute.

Writing sentences 2

Sentences need to make sense.

Walks love dogs. ✗   Dogs love walks. ✔

Q1 Copy the sentences that make sense.

The ice feels cold.
The boy in stream.
Dan forgot his book.
The shop sells sweets.
Ran as fast as he can.

_____

_____

_____

Q2 Look at this picture.
Write three sentences about it.

_____

_____

_____

Give your child a subject you know they find interesting, e.g. a pet. Ask them to write five sentences about the subject. Check it is punctuated properly.

Commas are used in lists.

crisps, sandwich, apple, chocolate, drink

Look carefully at where the commas are.

Q1 Add the missing commas to the lists.

spring summer autumn winter

red blue green black yellow white

car bus bicycle train boat

Q2 Sort the words in the box into lists.
(Hint: Some words may go into more than one list!)

floats   teachers   towels   stamps   packages   water
goggles   books   displays   children   till   postmaster

Things you find at a school:

_____

Things you find at a swimming pool:

_____

Things you find at a post office:

_____

Ask your child to write a very long shopping list with all their favourite foods — check they use commas correctly. Remember — no comma is required before the final 'and'.

Singular and plural 1

Nouns can be **singular** or **plural**.

Singular means *one*.

cat

Plural means *more than one*.

cats

You add **s** to many singular nouns to make them plural.

Q1 Write these nouns as plural nouns.

dog _____   duck _____

pig _____   cow _____

hen _____   spider _____

frog _____   owl _____

Q2 Circle the singular nouns in blue.
Circle the plural nouns in red.

books   nut   rat   cups   bird

hats   shed   shells   drinks   jumper

Remind your child what a noun is. Ask them to look through their reading book in search of plural nouns. Can they find ten where an 's' is added?

Nouns are naming words.
Proper nouns are nouns that are the name of something, like a person, a day, a month or a place.

Jay went to **Magicland** on **Tuesday**.

Proper nouns always start with a capital letter.

Q1 Look carefully at these nouns.
Copy the proper nouns. **Remember** to add the missing capital letters.

fish   sunday   jumper   november   jake   truck

london   table   bank   laila   dog   india

_____   _____   _____

_____   _____   _____

Q2 Copy these sentences correctly.

I am going to veejay's house on friday.

_____

helen is going to america on monday.

_____

The oxford street lights were put on in december.

_____

How am I doing?

Q1 Sort these words into the table.
Remember the missing capital letters.

towel   write   kite   wales   dance   lion

run   cinderella   ben   kick   newspaper   thursday

Nouns	Proper nouns	Verbs

Q2 Write these sentences correctly.
Remember capital letters, full stops, commas and question marks.

march comes before april

_____

what time shall we meet

_____

don't forget to bring sweets crisps apples

_____

can tom come to baker park too

_____

Every sentence starts with a **capital letter**.
Most sentences end with a **full stop**.

The baby crawled into the garden**.**

Q1 Use the words in the boxes to write your own sentences.

> **Friday   swimming   school**

_____

> **lion   sleep   tree**

_____

> **sweets   shop   buy**

_____

Q2 Look at this picture.
Write three sentences about it.

_____

_____

_____

Joining sentences 1

Two short **sentences** can be joined when a word is added between them.

The lorry moved too fast. It knocked over a wall.
The lorry moved too fast **and** it knocked over a wall.

Short sentences can be joined with the word **and**.

Q1 Join the two short sentences with the word **and**.

The leaves fell off the tree. They were raked into a pile.

_____

Zack forgot his coat. He forgot his school bag.

_____

The bird caught a worm. It took the worm back to its nest.

_____

Q2 Finish the sentences in your own words.

Jane was tired **and** _____

The sun is out **and** _____

The mouse ran away from the cat **and** _____

_____

Ask your child to find examples of sentences joined with the word 'and' in books at home.

Verbs 2

A **verb** is usually a doing word.
It tells us what is happening.

Tom **bakes** some cakes.

Q1 Write nine verbs.

Q2 Choose five of the verbs in **Q1** and write them into sentences.

_____

_____

_____

_____

_____

Ask your child to watch five minutes of television. While they are watching ask them to list every 'action' they see.

The **verbs** in a sentence must match the **nouns**.
If they don't the sentence doesn't make sense.

The **dog bark** at the cat.   *Doesn't make sense.*

The **dog barks** at the cat.   <u>*Does*</u> *make sense.*

Q1 Circle the verb in each sentence.

Maddie plays on the swing.

Tyler knocks over the glass.

The children run to the park.

The mouse eats the cheese.

Q2 Tick (✔) the sentences that make sense.
Cross (✘) the sentences that don't make sense.

I runs to the playground. ☐

The cakes cook for 20 minutes. ☐

Everyone love the film. ☐

Sarah walks to her friend's house. ☐

The dog lick my face. ☐

Write one of the wrong sentences correctly.

_____

It will help your child understand this topic if they know that a singular subject needs a single verb, a plural subject needs a plural verb.

Questions help us find out things.

Where are we going?

A question begins with a **capital letter** and ends with a **question mark**.

Q1 Write a question for each of these answers.

It is sunny and hot.

_____

You need to get up at 8 o'clock.

_____

My best friend is Rick.

_____

Q2 Look at this picture.
Write three of your own questions about it.

_____

_____

_____

Discuss different types of questions with your child. Closed questions can be answered with a 'yes' or 'no'. Open questions have a variety of different answers.

Proper nouns are nouns that are the <u>name</u> of something, like a person, a day, a month or a place.

Kate lives in **S**chool **L**ane, **R**odmart.

Q1 Copy these sentences correctly.

We love walking barney on exmoor.

_____

alex roberts was late for school on monday.

_____

italy is further away than france.

_____

Q2 Copy this address correctly.

mr james royman
61 carpenter road
crouch end
london
united kingdom

_____

_____

_____

_____

Ask your child to write as many proper nouns associated with him/herself as they can, e.g. name, pet names, road they live etc.

Exclamation marks

This is an **exclamation mark** !
It can be used at the end of a sentence
to show *shock, surprise, upset* or *an order.*

It's not fair!

Q1 Copy and add an exclamation mark to the sentences.

Watch out _____

Stop, thief _____

Quick, we have to hurry _____

This dead mouse stinks _____

Wow, look at that _____

Q2 Add a full stop, question mark or exclamation mark to these sentences.

Where is my hat_____

Ben won the race_____

I don't believe it_____

What time is it_____

Be quiet everyone_____

Highlight to your child that an exclamation mark is made with a full stop.

23

Singular and plural 2

Nouns can be **singular** or **plural**.

Singular means *one*.   **Plural** means *more than one*.

tent   tent**s**

You add **s** to many singular nouns to make them plural.

Q1 Underline the plural nouns in the sentences.

The rats eat the rabbit food.

Anil forgot his books for school.

Daisy collected water in her buckets.

The spades and forks were kept in the shed.

Cakes smell lovely after they come out of the oven.

Q2 Complete the sentences with plural nouns.
Use the singular nouns in the box to help.

chip   cat   trainer   burger   spider

The dog chased the _____.

Omar wore his _____ to school.

_____ often scare people.

Do you want _____ and _____ for tea tonight?

Challenge your child to find a noun for every letter of the alphabet that just needs an 's' added to it to make it plural.

24

Joining sentences 2

Two short **sentences** can be joined when a word is added between them.

The men built a fence. The wind blew it over.
The men built a fence **but** the wind blew it over.

Short sentences can be joined with the words **and** or **but**.

Q1 Add **and** or **but** to these sentences.

The dog fell in the river _____ it couldn't get out.

The red car is fast _____ the yellow car is faster.

Dan worked hard on his sums _____ he still got them wrong.

The cow slipped on the ice _____ she hurt her leg.

My numeracy is good _____ my literacy is better.

Q2 Finish the sentences in your own words.

Henry hurt himself **but** _____

The cat had six kittens **and** _____

Freya is happy **but** _____

The swimming pool was closed **but** _____

Matt worked hard **and** _____

Sentences can be joined with a number of different words. See if your child can find examples of different joining words in their reading book.

Nouns and verbs 2

Verbs in a sentence must match the **nouns**.
If they don't the sentence doesn't make sense.

The **snake slither** over the rock.   *Doesn't make sense.*

The **snake slithers** over the rock.   <u>Does</u> *make sense.*

Q1 Rewrite the sentences so that they make sense.

I can reads my book in bed.

_____

Meg eat her lunch quickly.

_____

Liam clap as the actors return.

_____

Q2 Use each noun in a sentence.
Make sure your sentence makes sense with the correct verb.
Underline the verb.

dog   _____

gate   _____

tiger   _____

Write some sentences but leave the noun out. Ask your child to correctly add a noun that agrees
with the verb in each sentence.

Commas are used in lists.

My favourite colours are red, yellow, green, blue and pink.

Look carefully at where the commas are.
A comma is *not* needed where the word **and** is used.

Q1 Add the missing commas to the sentences.

In a car you find keys maps seats and seatbelts.

In a house you find doors windows beds tables and chairs.

In a wardrobe you find coats shirts trousers dresses and shoes.

In a shed you find pots seeds spades forks and rakes.

Q2 Write these lists into your own sentences.

chips	dog	football
burger	sheep	tennis
drink	cows	running
apple	pigs	swimming

_____

_____

_____

Ask your child to write five sentences. In the first sentence ask them to use one comma, in the second sentence two commas and so on until they write a sentence with five commas.

Verbs – past tense

A **verb** is usually a doing word.
Some verbs tell us what has *already happened*.

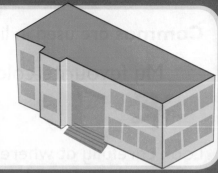

Andy **walked** to school.

The **verb** is in the **past tense**.

Q1 Add the past tense verbs to the sentences.

| kicked | baked | watched | played | visited |

We _____ Nan in hospital.

The cakes Najib _____ were tasty.

Yesterday we _____ a film.

Sonia _____ the ball at the window.

The toddler _____ in the mud.

Q2 Write each of these past tense verbs in a sentence.

saw _____

heard _____

felt _____

tasted _____

Give your child some short sentences written in the present, e.g. I brush my teeth, I watch television.
Ask them to write each of the sentences in the past tense, e.g. I brushed my teeth, I watched television.

Writing sentences 3

Sentences start with a **capital letter** and end with a **full stop** (.), **question mark** (?) or **exclamation mark** (!).

Q1 Read the passage and copy three sentences, one with a full stop, one with a question mark and one with an exclamation mark.

"When will we get there?" asked Tom. He was very tired after waking up early.
"Not long now," Mum replied.
Then everything went wrong.
"Look out, there is a cat in the road!" shouted Tom.
The car skidded to a stop, just missing the cat...

_____

_____

_____

Q2 Write a sentence with
a full stop

_____

a question mark

_____

an exclamation mark

_____

As extra practice, write some sentences that should end with full stops, question marks and exclamation marks. Ask your child to add the missing punctuation marks.

Q1 Write the **plural** of each of the nouns.

bee _____   chair _____

pen _____   spoon _____

banana _____   vest _____

Q2 Join the short sentences with **and** or **but**.

Tim played football. He scored a goal.

_____

Zoe ran up the road. She missed the bus.

_____

Annie fell over. She hurt her knee.

_____

Kyle forgot his bag. It didn't matter.

_____

Q3 Write four **past tense verbs**.
Remember the past tense is when something has already happened.

_____   _____

_____   _____

Q4 Fill each gap with a **verb**.

The children _____ a story.

Aimee _____ her flute.

Daniel _____ his breakfast.

Mr Morris _____ at the dog.

Q5 Copy the **proper nouns** correctly.

new york   jumper   austria   sandwich

zoo   meena   september   computer

_____   _____

_____   _____

Q6 Write these sentences correctly.
Remember capital letters, full stops, commas, question marks and exclamation marks.

we have run out of time

_____

when can I cook tea

_____

I need to go to tetbury to buy milk eggs butter and bread

_____

Answers

Capital letters
Page 4
1 A B **C** D E F **G** H I J K **L** M N O **P** Q R **S** T U V W **X** Y Z

2 It is a hot day.

The dog sat on a cat.

We like sweets.

Full stops
Page 5
1 The pool is fun.

A girl plays tennis.

Dan walks to school.

The hen laid an egg.

2 Child to complete sentences ending with a full stop.

Nouns
Page 6
1 boat, tree, chair, dog, ring, sun

2 Child to list nouns s/he can see around them.

Proper nouns
Page 7
1 The following words circled:

Meena, London, Ben, Africa, Cinderella, Tonkin Road, Mr Atkin, France

2 Child's answers to questions using proper nouns.

Capital letters and full stops 1
Page 8
1 It is raining.

We love sweets.

Sam is swimming.

2 Child's own sentences using the following words:

dog stick, baby food, lion sleep

Writing sentences 1
Page 9
1 Cats sleep anywhere.

Children splash in the puddles. / The children splash in puddles.

The car is grey.

2 e.g. We are going on holiday.

e.g. The teacher is grumpy.

e.g. The lion bites the zookeeper.

Verbs
Page 10
1 eating, cycling, laughing, skiing, slipping, standing

2 Child lists verbs of actions they have done that day.

Questions 1
Page 11
1 Where are you going?

Why is your coat muddy?

When can I eat my snack?

What is his name?

2 Three questions written by child.

Writing sentences 2
Page 12
1 The ice feels cold.

Dan forgot his book.

The shop sells sweets.

2 Child to write three sentences about picture.

Commas in lists 1
Page 13
1 spring, summer, autumn, winter

red, blue, green, black, yellow, white

car, bus, bicycle, train, boat

2 Things you find at a school: teachers, water, books, displays, children

Things you find at a swimming pool: floats, towels, water, goggles, till, children

Things you find at a post office: packages, till, postmaster, children, stamps

Singular and plural 1
Page 14
1 dogs ducks pigs cows hens spiders frogs owls

2 The following words circled in blue: shed nut rat jumper bird

The following words circled in red: hats books shells drinks cups

Nouns and proper nouns 1
Page 15
1 Sunday, November, Jake, London, Laila, India

2 I am going to Veejay's house on Friday.

Helen is going to America on Monday.

The Oxford Street lights were put on in December.

How am I doing?
Page 16
1

Nouns	Proper nouns	Verbs
towel	Thursday	run
newspaper	Wales	kick
kite	Ben	write
lion	Cinderella	dance

2 March comes before April.

What time shall we meet?

Don't forget to bring sweets, crisps, apples.

Can Tom come to Baker Park too?

Capital letters and full stops 2
Page 17
1 Child's own sentences correctly punctuated with capital letter and full stop using the following words:

Friday, swimming, school

lion, sleep, tree

sweets, shop, buy

2 Three of child's own sentences about the picture.

Joining sentences 1
Page 18
1 The leaves fell off the tree and they were raked into a pile.

Zack forgot his coat and he forgot his school bag.

The bird caught a worm and it took the worm back to its nest.

2 Child to finish three sentences in own words.

Verbs 2
Page 19
1 Child's choice of nine verbs.

2 Child asked to write five words from **Q1** into their own sentences.